D1154560

A School Album

Peter and Connie Roop

Heinemann Library
Des Plaines, Illinois

Designed by Lindaanne Donohoe
Printed in Hong Kong

03 02 01 00 99
10 9 8 7 6 5 4 3 2

Library of Congress Cataloging-in-Publication Data
Roop, Peter
    A School album / Peter and Connie Roop.
       p.   cm. — (Long ago and today)
    Includes bibliographical references and index.
    Summary: Text, photographs, and illustrations identify and trace
patterns of change and continuity in American schools, covering such
topics as travel to school, subjects studied, and the nature of the
classrooms.
    ISBN 1-57572-603-3 (lib. bdg.)
    1. Elementary schools—United States—History—Juvenile
literature. 2. Education, Elementary—United States—History
—Juvenile literature. (1. Schools—History.) I. Roop, Connie.
II. Title. III. Series: Roop, Peter. Long ago and today.
LA219.R66   1998
372.973'09—dc21   98-17899
                                                                            CIP
                                                                            AC

Acknowledgments
The authors and publishers are grateful to the following for permission to reproduce
copyright photographs:

Cover photographs: Stock Montage, Inc., top; Phil Martin, bottom
Corbis-Bettmann, pp. 8, 10, 12,16 back cover right; Stock Montage, Inc.; pp. 4, 5, 6, 14, 20, 22
top; Steve Benbow, pp. 15, 17; Phil Martin, pp. 7, 9, 11, 13, 19, 21, 22 bottom, back cover left;
Culver Pictures, Inc., p.18.

Grateful acknowledgement to Mrs. June G. Shackter, principal
of Stephen Decatur Classical School, Chicago, Illinois.

Every effort has been made to contact copyright holders of any material reproduced in this
book. Any omissions will be rectified in subsequent printings if notice is given to the publisher.

Some words are shown in bold, **like this.** You can find out what they mean by looking
in the glossary.

For Judy—In appreciation for your leadership and friendship.
        You are truly an inspired teacher!

Contents

The School

one-room log schoolhouse

A long time ago, many children went to school. They learned to read, to write, and do math. Students had fun during recess and lunch. They sang, drew, and exercised. But not all children went to school.

Some children worked in factories, **mines,** or on farms. Few African American children went to school. School lasted only five months because children were needed at home to help with chores. Most students stopped going to school at the end of eighth grade. Today all children must go to school.

children working in the family garden

Getting to School

Long ago, most students lived on farms or in small towns. They walked to school. A few lucky students rode horses or in wagons. They hurried because if they were late, they had to wait outside until recess.

Many students had long walks to school, often in snow.

About 50 students can ride to school on one school bus.

Today, students still walk to school. Many more ride in cars, buses, or **subways.** Many children ride bikes, too. Students still hurry to get to school before the bell rings.

Outside the School

children playing outside a one-room schoolhouse, 1860

Long ago, most schools were built of wood. One or two windows let in a little light. Some schools had an **outhouse** for a restroom. Few had a **well** for water. A fireplace or wood stove heated the school.

Today, most schools are in cities and towns. Schools are built of steel and brick. Windows and electric lights light up the rooms. Schools have restrooms inside. Schools are heated by large **furnaces** that burn oil, gas, or use electricity.

children playing outside a large school, 1998

A Classroom

Classrooms were small and teachers sat at the front of the class.

Long ago schools had one room with many grades crowded in. Students sat on wood benches or desks. Maps were put on the walls.

Classrooms are larger today, with a lot of room to move about.

Today, there are only students of one grade in a room. There are many grades in the whole school. Students sit at desks and tables. Rooms are bright and colorful and have the students' work hanging on walls and from the ceiling.

Reading and Writing

For writing lessons, many students wrote on *slate* tablets.

Long ago reading lessons were noisy. Students read out loud at the same time. There were very few books and no libraries. If the school had paper, students wrote with **quill pens** and ink.

Today, students read stories out loud to the teacher or a partner. They also read silently to themselves. There are many books in classrooms. Most schools have their own libraries. Pencils and paper or computers are used for writing.

*Today's students use computers to publish their own books and to get information from CD-ROMs and the **Internet.***

Art and Music

Math facts or poems were sung to a tune like "Yankee Doodle."

Long ago, songs were part of a math or reading lesson. Teachers gave few art lessons. Many students liked to draw on their **slates.** Some even carved pictures into their benches.

These students are learning to play the recorder.

Today, many schools have art and music classes. Students learn how to draw, paint, and make things during art class. In music, they learn musical notes and how to play instruments and to sing.

Recess

Winslow Homer's painting, Snap the Whip, *1872*

Long ago, recess was a time to run and have fun. Children played around the school house. Boys played games like marbles, tag, or snap the whip. Girls played jacks, jump rope, or chase. Laughter rang across the schoolyard during recess.

Today, students play basketball, football, soccer, four square, baseball, tag, jump rope, and many other playground games. Some playgrounds are grassy. Others are paved. Boys and girls often play together.

playground with swings, climbing bars, and game areas, 1998

Lunchtime

Lunch was often eaten outside when the weather was good and in the classroom when it rained or snowed.

Long ago, students brought their lunches to school in a pail or in their pockets. They ate fresh bread with homemade jam or meat. In winter, a hot potato kept cold hands warm on the way to school and then was eaten at lunch.

Today, students still bring lunches from home. Sandwiches, chips, cookies, and fruit are packed in lunch bags or lunch boxes. Many students eat hot meals cooked at school. After eating, they go outside to play.

*Today, students eat in a **cafeteria** or a gym.*

Math and Science

Students wrote math problems on their **slates.** Teachers gave math problems which students did in their heads. Students only did a little science in school. They learned about nature from the woods, water, and farms around them.

students learning about how people breathe, 1889.

students learning about bones, 1998

Today, students use paper, pencils, and books to do math. They use **calculators** and computers to practice. Growing things, making models, and doing experiments are part of today's science class.

Going Home

Long ago, students hurried home after school to do their chores. Just like students today, they were tired from school, but they had learned something, too.

Glossary

cafeteria lunchroom where people choose food and bring it to tables to eat

calculator machine like a computer that solves math problems

furnaces machines that heat homes and buildings

Internet group of computers connected together

mines large holes or tunnels in the earth where special rocks or materials are dug

outhouse small building outdoors that has a toilet

quill pens pens made from bird feathers

slate thin piece of rock that is used to write on, like a small chalkboard

subways trains that can travel underground

well deep hole in the ground where water is brought out

More Books to Read

Birnbaum, Bette. *My School, Your School.* Austin, Tex: Raintree Steck-Vaughn, 1990.

Greene, Carol. *At the School.* Plymouth, Minn: Child's World, 1998.

Kalman, Bobbie. *A One Room School.* New York: Crabtree, 1994.

Index